MUSHROOMS AND FUNGI

By
Robin Twiddy

FOREST EXPLORER

BookLife PUBLISHING

©2018
BookLife Publishing
King's Lynn
Norfolk PE30 4LS

All rights reserved.
Printed in Malaysia.

A catalogue record for this book is available from the British Library.

ISBN: 978-1-78637-477-6

Written by:
Robin Twiddy

Edited by:
Kirsty Holmes

Designed by:
Gareth Liddington

Photocredits: All images are courtesy of Shutterstock.com.

Cover – Fotofermer, hddigital, valzan, EtiAmmos, Chantal de Bruijne, Videopoint, Andrey Jitkov, 1 - diamant24, 2 - allstars, 3 - Yogamreet, 4 - attila, 5 - drpnncpptak, specnaz, Jalisko, 6 - Monkey Business Images, Denis508, 7 - Maria Evseyeva, 8 - PHOTO FUN, 9 - Polia 111, 10 - Nadia Brusnikova, 11 - Elina Yevgrashkina, 12 - LaineN, 13 - Hatchapong Palurtchaivong, 14 - Barry Blackburn, 15 - photo_pw, 16 - Michal Ninger, 17 - Charles Gammon, 18 - Mike Nash, 19 - Nitr, Isabel Eve, 20 - Dora Zett, 21 - aing1970, 22 - KateMacate, 23 - Arie v.d. Wolde, wavebreakmedia.

Images are courtesy of Shutterstock.com. With thanks to Getty Images, Thinkstock Photo and iStockphoto.

All facts, statistics, web addresses and URLs in this book were verified as valid and accurate at time of writing. No responsibility for any changes to external websites or references can be accepted by either the author or publisher.

CONTENTS

Words that look like **this** can be found in the glossary on page 24.

Page 4	Let's Explore
Page 5	Grab Your Equipment
Page 6	Being Careful
Page 8	What Are Mushrooms and Fungi?
Page 10	Where Do They Grow?
Page 12	Seasons
Page 14	Types of Fungi
Page 16	Which Animals Eat Mushrooms?
Page 18	What Fungi Do in the Forest
Page 20	Picking Mushrooms
Page 22	Keeping Notes
Page 24	Glossary and Index

LET'S EXPLORE

WELCOME, FOREST EXPLORER!

Today we will be looking for mushrooms and fungi. We will learn what they are, what they look like and where to find them.

GRAB YOUR EQUIPMENT

A budding forest explorer will need:

Camera

Magnifying Glass

Notebook

Walking Boots

BEING CAREFUL

Before we begin exploring the forest, it is important that we know how to be safe. Always make sure you have an adult explorer with you.

Although some mushrooms are **edible**, some are very harmful if you eat them. Be safe, and leave the mushrooms where you found them.

WHAT ARE MUSHROOMS AND FUNGI?

Slime Mould

Fungi are not plants or animals; they are another type of life. The **kingdom** of fungi includes mushrooms and mould.

Mushrooms are the **fruiting** part of a fungus, like a conker on a tree. Mushrooms don't have babies, or drop seeds. Instead they release **spores**.

Boletus Mushroom

WHERE DO THEY GROW?

Fungi generally like to grow in damp areas. They also like to grow on their food, such as on a tree or a rotting log.

These honey mushrooms are growing on a tree with some damp moss.

Mushrooms grow in lots of different sizes, shapes, colours and patterns. Some grow very slowly and some grow very fast.

SEASONS

Some mushrooms grow in different seasons.
Other mushrooms can be found all year round in the forest.

Try taking notes about the mushrooms you find in your forest in the summer. Are the same mushrooms there in the winter?

Go to page 22 to learn about taking notes.

TYPES OF FUNGI

There are lots of types of fungi. Mushrooms and toadstools are just one type. Sac fungi is another type. They grow in strange and curly shapes.

Truffles are a very rare sac fungi used for cooking.

The lichen on this tree is part plant and part fungi.

Some fungi do not grow mushrooms and live under the soil or on tree bark. There are even some fungi that live in animal stomachs and help them **digest** food.

WHICH ANIMALS EAT MUSHROOMS?

Lots of forest animals love to eat wild mushrooms. Some big animals that eat mushrooms are: badgers, deer, pigs and rabbits.

Some smaller animals that eat mushrooms in the forest are: squirrels, mice, slugs, ants, termites and other insects.

This squirrel is enjoying a large mushroom.

WHAT FUNGI DO IN THE FOREST

Fungi play an important role in the forest. Fungi feed off the parts of leaves and trees that don't rot.

This fungi is feeding off the fallen leaves.

Lots of fungi are working to break down this fallen branch.

When fungi eat the old leaves and fallen trees, they put lots of **nutrients** back into the soil. This helps the forest grow and stay healthy.

PICKING MUSHROOMS

SOME MUSHROOMS CAN MAKE YOU SICK IF YOU TOUCH THEM. CHECK WITH AN **EXPERT** FIRST.

Many people go mushroom-picking in the forest. If you do, make sure that you have an adult with you who can **identify** which mushrooms you are picking.

Some mushrooms are very **poisonous**, and it is better to be safe than sorry. Use your magnifying glass to get a good look instead of picking them.

Keep a **record** of the mushrooms you see.

KEEPING NOTES

When you do see mushrooms while exploring, it is important to keep careful notes. This way you will be able to identify them later.

You can note the colour, size and special markings of the mushroom.

Mushrooms and fungi are very interesting when you look carefully. Maybe you will discover a new type in your forest. What would you call it?

GLOSSARY

digest	to break down food into things that can be absorbed and used by the body
edible	safe to be eaten
expert	an adult who knows a lot about a topic
fruiting	the part of the plant that contains seeds or the part of a fungi that contains spores
identify	spot or recognise
kingdom	the large division of things into animal, plant or fungi
nutrients	natural substances that plants and animals need to grow and stay healthy
poisonous	dangerous or deadly when eaten
record	keeping track of something

INDEX

expert 20
insects 17
leaves 18–19
lichen 15
magnifying glass 5, 21

mould 8
poison 21
rot 10, 18
sac fungi 14
spores 9

summer 13
trees 9–10, 15, 18–19
truffles 14
winter 13